THE HOT ICE CREAM EMPIRE

R. Nikolas Macioci

ISBN: 978-81-19654-86-4

First Edition: 2024
Rs. 200/-

Cyberwit.net
HIG 45 Kaushambi Kunj, Kalindipuram
Allahabad - 211011 (U.P.) India
http://www.cyberwit.net
Tel: +(91) 9415091004
E-mail: info@cyberwit.net

Printed at Repro India Limited.

To Henry Coleman, one of God's perfect people
who always spreads his arms extra wide to show
me how much he likes my writing and for whom
I open my arms extra wide to show him how
how much I care

Acknowledgments

Grateful acknowledgement is made to the following publications in which some of these poems first appeared:

“Appraising the Parade of Homes” *Fresh Words*

“Mirror” *Fresh Words*

“After the Drums” *Fresh Words*

“The Girl Who Married Me Without My Consent” *Ginosko Literary Journal*

“A Vulnerable Choice at Vermilion, Ohio” *Ginosko Literary Journal*

“No Holiday” *Ginosko Literary Journal*

“Glass Knives” *Ginosko Literary Journal*

“Simplified Breakup” *Ginosko Literary Journal*

“The Myth of Mozart’s Common Grave” *Tipton Poetry Journal*

“Hustler’s Sport” *Moria Literary Magazine*

“Sometimes life is just what it is, and
the best thing you can hope for is ice cream.”

Abbi Waxman, *Other People’s Houses*

Contents

PART ONE

THE HOT ICE CREAM EMPIRE

Mom's in our confectionery, dipping
ice cream. I loiter beside her, ask
why freezers are so cold? With head still down,
she spurts, *Don't expect them to be hot do you?*
For an eight-year-old you ask the dumbest
questions. Go play somewhere. At the front
counter, Dad gabs with a customer.

I trudge to the back room where an old,
upright piano would beg for a tune-up
if it could talk. Earlier, Dad unpacked supplies,
left several, large, cardboard boxes for me
to tear apart, set fire to in the alley. I plop
onto the piano bench, use my right hand
to pick out "Tennessee Waltz," Mom's favorite.
Bored, I stare at three, oversized boxes.
I'll make a house out of one of them.
Dad's toolbox is on the table across the room.
I retrieve an X-Acto knife, cut a door
in the biggest box, wiggle inside.
Semi dark surrounds me, but I feel safe,
wish I felt this way at home. No screaming
arguments, knife threats, gunshots through
kitchen floor threaten me here.

Next thing I know, the entire box shakes.
Kick after kick collapses the side. Dad yells,
Get out. Why wasn't I in the alley
incinerating it instead of sitting in it.

I crawl out to a slap that burns like a claw mark,
tears withheld. Alcoholic breath orders me
to the alley. I rip the box to pieces, lug them
outside. I strike a match, a little boy
whose drunken Dad has deliberately
destroyed two houses.

LESSON OF THE SNOW MOON

The city disappears, obliterated
by continual snow. I breathe through a scarf
wrapped around my face, fur-lined gloves
not enough to keep hands warm. Access
to my house is impassable unless I clear
the driveway. I've been heaping snow as high
as I can for over an hour, feel as if I were
excavating to find asphalt.

I stop shoveling, a foot of snow, white
as cottage cheese, banked on either side
of the driveway. This is the month of many snows.
It's only the middle of February, and, so far,
three blizzards have buried landscape, crippled
drivers, turned what is familiar into the unidentifiable.

I look at the seventy-foot, maple tree silvered by icy snow.
The orange moon reaches me through overlapping
branches. For some reason, I think of marriage,
and words come to mind: touch, hope, despair.
I didn't cry when my parents divorced because
Mom and I were freed from a man with dark circles
under his eyes bent on abusing us.

It begins to snow again. I can't control constant
accumulation just as I couldn't the over-enthusiastic thwacks
of my dad's belt.

I bend at the waist, resume routine of shoveling.
I wish the moon wouldn't follow me, or so it seems,
the same moon under which Dad's capacity to love shriveled,
the same moon under which he held arms at his sides,
the closest he ever got to hugging me.

SWIMMING THROUGH LEAVES

Dad slumps on a bar stool in Sweeney's
beer joint. I leave my 7UP half finished,
go outside where I can almost taste surprise
of October sun. A giant, maple tree
overhangs the cafe. Leaves, red
as a ladybug, have piled beneath the tree.

I escape Dad's boozy breath, wrap
my seven-year-old body in leaves,
wish myself away from merciless cruelty,
the stinging belt he sometimes whips
from his waist with drunken hands.
I dive deep into God's scarlet handiwork,
make snow-angel movements until
I feel elsewhere.

The door flies open. He wobbles
from the cafe as if he'd knocked wind
out of himself, lumbers toward me.
Leaves continue to fall like fluttering
handkerchiefs. I rise to my feet, anticipate
wild bite of his belt, but he's too drunk
to follow through. Instead, he grips my arm,
pushes me in the direction of our house
two blocks away. I've escaped punishment
by default. The belt will come later,
his version of an embrace.

SOUTH 6TH STREET

After a storm, we shaped earth to suit us.
Braxton and Bradley, twin brothers, and I
would drop everything, meet on 6th Street
where muddy water had accumulated
in tempting puddles. We were seven
years old, and in the 1940s, neighborhood
kids could play on side streets and alleys
without fear of traffic.

On this particular day, we banked mud,
built harbors, floated boats made of popsicle
sticks. We steered a course with second grade
seamanship. Barefoot or sandaled like
Biblical shepherds, we played until
my dad tromped into view. I could almost
smell anger wafting from him. Whenever
he had to look for me for supper, his belt hung
from a tight fist like indisputable damnation.
I unfolded from my knees, pled for forgiveness.
He scooted me home.

As we approached the house, the scent of
fried potatoes escaped through a summer,
screen door. Mom fussed in the kitchen,
setting the table. She would mediate because
I had no excuse to offer but innocence.

THAT NIGHT

My dad, nicknamed Shorty, killed me
in many ways. When he drank, he transformed
into a man mean as a rabid monkey.
He liked ladies in excess, and for that reason,
alone, should never have married or had children.
At twenty-one, he and his tireless work ethic rose
to superintendent of Federal Glass Company.
Of all the girls on the assembly line, hand painting
Scottie dogs onto juice glasses, he focused on Mom,
asked for a date. Shortly afterwards, the farm girl
married the handsome Sicilian.

I always wondered what had hurt him
to cause alcoholism and to abuse Mom and me.
I couldn't see it in his eyes. I couldn't see anything
in his eyes but the color of expensive, milk chocolate.

The night he almost lost his infant son,
he had taken Mom, her sister, Liz, and Liz's husband,
Toots to play cards at the Grotskys, friends of Liz
and Toots. The Grotskys lived two steps shy
of tar paper houses. It was 1941, and they were proud
to afford any kind of house. Actually, cheap, green
shingles topped their roof. The Grotskys glowed
with warmth and hospitality. Continual refills
of beer accompanied the poker game.
After several hands, Mom found herself
unable to balance me on her lap while playing,
so she faded to a heavily nicked, wooden, rocking chair.

My two-month-old head lay close to the chair's arm.
Dad tottered from the card game, slurred words,
"You're spoiling that baby." He whipped out
a pocket knife, opened the blade, took aim.
The knife sliced air, stuck in the chair arm
an inch from my head. He laughed, turned back
to the card table.

As I grew up, Mom told me this story many times,
and we agreed that fate and drunken focus
had saved me from being a surefire fatality.

THROUGH THE EMPTY STREETS

Title taken from the poem "He Thinks
He Can Leave Me" by Saeed Jones

The son fingers a pocket knife in his jeans,
wishes he could slash his dad's alcoholism
out of existence. Angry, the nine-year-old
trudges down Parsons Avenue, peering
into bars to find his dad. It's 10:00 at night.
He lumbers past conspicuous prostitutes,
notes their rehearsed smiles beneath neon.
His mom is working in their confectionery.
Dad is supposed to be delivering beer.

The son turns down a side street to an alley,
pees, shivers, zips up. His patience, like a
shoe sole, wears thin. He resumes the hunt,
the last place on this well-worn route, Gavins.
He pushes through smoke, finds Dad humped
on a stool. "Mom wants you to come home."
A middle-age redhead leans over, says,
"Who is this, Honey." Duty done,

the son doesn't wait to ride home with his
tipsy Dad, bolts from the bar, takes larger
than nine-year-old steps to the confectionery.
He knows a secret his mom doesn't: soon,
Dad will stumble to a room in his sister's
house accompanied be another woman.
He will report to his mom where his dad is,

but he will not mention the scene
he once stumbled upon in his aunt's house.

He pulls the knife from his pocket, lacerates
air as he hastens away from drunken breath
and everything he wishes he didn't know.

OFF THE PLAYING FIELD

Sun blazed down on my nine-year-old back
the day I sidestepped recreation period
at Camp St. Joseph. I trudged toward woods,
away from embarrassment for never having
learned the game of baseball.

Sagging down against a gigantic oak,
I listened to excited shouts and the clunk
when bat and ball made contact. I wanted to be
home, miles from the dusty field bleached
from stifling sunlight.

Thinking I had sliced my wrists by walking
away from the game, I further risked returning
to my cabin, a two-room, log structure, windows
propped open with hacked-off broom handles. I
stayed low, stooped back to irresistible solitude.

Before I could reach the cabin, my counselor
rounded the corner, his facial accusation blocked me,
straddled escape. His ox head tilted from a stump neck.
Captive to his stubborn eyes, I stood still and silent.
His unsympathetic look held me steadfast as I listened

to words I will never forget. *I hate a sneak.*
Venom in his voice engulfed me. I felt suffocated.
With a brisk heel turn, he disappeared, left me shamed.
I stayed wrapped in the cabin's shadow for several minutes,
thinking how I couldn't bring myself to stop him

by admitting I had never learned to throw a ball.

RAW WISDOM

I awake mid-dream, alone.
Parents trusted I would sleep until morning.
With seven-year-old determination, I slip
out of bed, from the house, determined
to find the confectionery my parents own and run.

I amble to the first intersection, Hinman Avenue
and South 6th Street. It's 1948, traffic is minimal,
almost non-existent at this hour of the night, so
I stop in the middle of the street, look past streetlight
at sky. I stare at innumerable stars that appear
as white-hot as this July evening. I continue to gaze
upward. Something in the talking part of my head
tells me I know too much, more than a kid
my age should: an older boy seduced me
at the age of six in the attic part of his garage.
I heard my parents in the next bedroom making love,
thought they were hurting one another.
In a buffet drawer beneath a pile of doilies, I found
a picture of Snow White and the Seven Dwarfs
having sex.

I turn away from stars before I drown
in dangerous secrets. So little traffic passes
I can saunter down the center of the street
to my destination. I plan my story, hope
they will accept my leaving home by myself.
Mine is a story about intuition guiding me to them.
Mine is a story about stars holding me spellbound.

AFTER THE DRUMS

At eight years old, I watched the earth rip open,
thatched huts fold over fissures of ruptured ground.
Lana Turner, face contorted in horror, braced herself
in a doorway, poise untarnished despite the island's
undulations and a cast of thousands already dead.
After the earthquake, there was much kissing
between Lana and Van Heflin which I tried
to ignore by slumping down in my seat.

Mom had taken me with her to see
Green Dolphin Street at the Markham which
we walked twelve blocks to get to. I liked
the quake scene, but what followed gave me
bad dreams for weeks. On a moonless night,
in a hut shadowed by black Palms, Lana and
her young daughter huddled in bed waiting
for a Maori attack. Drums thumped, thumped,
thumped in endless repetition. Suddenly,
they stopped. Ten seconds passed without sound,
nothing but deadly silence. Lana hugged her child,
marking time. Then, it happened. An instantaneous
stream of black bodies jumped through the window,
over the bed, and out the opposite window.
It looked as if the shape of a black rainbow streamed
across the bed. I shivered. The scene traumatized me.
Even though Heflin sprang through the door,
brow furrowed, eyes bulging with concern, and held
Lana and her daughter until daylight, I left the theater
feeling as if my safety had been slashed by a machete.

In bed that night, I listened for the constant drum beat,
for terrifying stillness that would follow
the drums' abrupt stop, and then the terrifying danger
that would arc across my bed for the rest of my life.

MIRROR

On a particular, August afternoon,
I sauntered through the field from my house
to Aunt Mary's. My mom's sister had two boys,
I had shaken off adolescence, the way a dog does
unwelcome water, by spending every chance I got
with her sons. We were closer than many brothers,
inseparable. We exhausted Parker board games,
clipped coupons from comic books with guaranteed
promises of pocket radios and walkie talkies,
neither of which actually existed yet, but we sent
money and hope, waited for each day's mail.

As I approached Aunt Mary's house on this specific,
August day, I noticed the car as well as Aunt Mary
and the boys were gone. The back door had been left
open. A person could do that in the 1950s
when folks were still connoisseurs of trust.
I entered past the unlatched screen door, made a tour
to confirm no one was there. In the living room,
on an impulse, I glanced, over my shoulder
at the mirror mounted above the fireplace.
I could not believe myself at that moment.
It was as if I had metamorphosed
from an ordinary adolescent into one who could stand
with pride alongside the kid in the Coke ad. I
knew instinctively time would taint this bit of ego.
In fact, I wouldn't have been surprised if
someone had stepped into the room and said,
"It will not last forever."

I'll go home, I thought, try not to leave
newfound confidence behind.

As I shut the screen door, I reasoned maybe
it had been a trick of the light. After all,
many people are perfect at seventeen.

IMPARTIAL HEALING

Dr Phillips is younger than I am,
ignores me each time I take Aunt Liz
to see this respiratory specialist
for her pulmonary fibrosis.
She slumps on the end of the examining table,
tries to hold the open-back, hospital gown shut.
He glances past me, eyes the color of a jay,
presses the stethoscope's diaphragm
to her chest, checks blood pressure, scribbles
a prescription for Cipro, disappears
from a whip-sharp turn at the door.
Aunt Liz and I look at each other, comment
on the appointment's brevity. She likes
the doctor, but fifteen minutes is
the allowable time slot.

After she re-dresses in the adjoining bathroom,
we take the elevator to the ground floor.
I tell her to wait in the lobby until I bring the car
from the parking garage. It has snowed all day.
I'm worried she will slip walking from the building
to the car. It is too long a journey for her to amble
with me to the garage. I pull the car around
to the front of the hospital, climb out, trudge
through unshoveled snow to the lobby, take her arm.
We totter careful steps to the car.

On the way home, she blurts, "I'm not ready to die."
Catching my breath, I swallow, not wanting to broach

a cruel subject, possibly one close at hand.
It's snowing harder. It's as if we are locked in
a white room. I turn to her and say,
"You're going to be around a long, long time."
We are silent then. Windshield wipers brush slush aside,
clear our way home.

EXCHANGES

The birthday gift I plan to exchange
lies on the back seat of my car.
I dwell unshaven, deep in warmth
of a gray sweatshirt, drive down South
High Street to the shopping center.
I'm humming a song to myself when
I hear revved engine roar beside me.
The cop zooms his motorcycle past,
a detached look on his face as he guns
toward the center lane. In rearview
mirror I see the funeral procession he leads.
I swerve toward curb, wait. A limousine
follows the cop. I assume its passengers
brim with Saturday sorrow. Through
the window of one of the cortege cars,
I spot preteen heads. Perhaps they are still
learning protocol for disposing of a body,
stunned or fascinated with the ritual's
dismal pageantry.

A black flag flaps on the last car.
I resume driving, still able to spot
the methodical parade. I feel heavy
as a ream of wet paper, have lost desire
for song, the need to exchange a birthday
present. Up ahead, the procession continues
its slow pace toward eternity, and as if
put there for irony, I pass a billboard
that reads "Guess Who's Coming Home?"

THE GIRL WHO MARRIED ME WITH-OUT MY CONSENT

It's obvious you're trying to kill me
by taking me into your life
as a pseudo husband. I keep my head down
to avoid volumes of subtext that flies
at me like furious birds. I don't trust
your ordinary words to be ordinary.
What a bad novel our lives would make,
you waiting in the wings for a morsel
of physical contact, I sidestepping the life
I want while trying to maintain only
a friendship. I'm flattered you would take me
in any condition, place me on the shelf
of your expectations much like a taxidermist
stuffs sawdust into an animal to keep it around.

You want my time like a kid down the block did
when I was ten years old. He had enticements,
board games, marbles, a baseball glove.
We would sit opposite each other, wait
for the gleam that was supposed to happen
between friends. He was radiant
in an adolescent way. I loved him
for putting zing in my life. One day,
we promised to meet. I wasted the whole
afternoon waiting for him. He didn't show up,
and I never saw him again.
His was the kind of love I want.

I'm not a kid anymore to be lured
by toy trucks, trains, or self-serving kindness.
I don't want security you entice me with,
the tacit insinuation of happiness ever after
lurking in everything you do for me.
Your wish for more than a friendship is blatant
as a vacation brochure. Why shouldn't I be alone?
Is there anything as lush, as grand, as
cemetery-kind-of-grief that gives loneliness
its special greatness? I'd rather be sad
than committed to the wrong person.
Sadness is good. I'm sure of it.
Didn't you really know I was someone else
all along? I want you to step over here,
shake my hand, allow us to part.
I need the time. I have poetry to write.

SIMPLIFIED BREAKUP

I search for talk that will not make me sound
like the person you are leaving. You fold
your clothes into boxes. I separate anything
of mine that clutters your effort. You will
go to another part of the city, take a room,
feel someone else's shoulder under your hand.

I used to do your laundry, some t-shirts
threadbare, stained. You stack the boxes
by the door, and it comforts me to swallow
a sarcastic laugh. I reduce all of this to
first caring words you repeated over and over,
convincing me I should disorder my life

for another person. Say those words again,
if you can remember. I tell you it is all I want.
It is all I will keep. Say them, so I can never
mistake the truth one more time. Say them,
so I will be a little less aggrieved when I awaken.
You crushed commitment to the relationship

as ruthlessly as an autumn wind tears leaves
from trees. What did it all mean? Like religion,
you were an incomparable model of certainty.
You don't remember those words, do you?
Those words belonged only to one evening
as I feared they would. The small favor I ask,

so far from that beginning, is that you recall
those words. I want to hear the discrepancy
between what you said and the deed,
a discrepancy like fake roses I can sit on
my nightstand and study for sobering effect.
Say them.

SIMILAR TO A KNIFE WOUND

I breathe air imbued with a coyote's howl.
I lounge on the porch of Aunt Ada's cabin
where I will stay by myself for a few days.
Yips, barks, and growls signal the presence
of coyote pups in the woods bordering
her property.

I step into the cabin away from false, April
warmth. I'm here, in this place of conclusions,
to heal from the end of a relationship.
I never learned behavior that protects
from the harm of romance. I flop onto the couch,
gaze out the window at muddy, creek water.

First days of infatuation flash through my brain,
bring me to the absurd, lifelong commitment
that lasted only three years, first moments,
so deceptive. Longing rippled my spine,
gorged my mind with extraordinary light
whenever I saw you. No sound will ever hurt
as much as your voice admitting heroin addiction.
Helplessness melted down to my toes like snow
in the blood. I wanted to vanish, take back time
wasted.

I turn into the room, glad not to be starved
for your return. Because this is not the city,
there isn't a sidewalk to look out on for strangers.
Only woods loom and eerie quiet like a funeral
home where inconsolable apparitions are put
to rest, and the smell of rotting roses permeates.

JOURNEY TO IMMORTALITY

Mom and I have packed luggage
into the maroon, 1953 Chevy,
head to St. Augustine. Our second,
stopping-off place, Scenic View Motel
in Homestead.

After checking in, we drive to a nearby
restaurant, Chaney's, a mile down the road.
The waitress, a thin lady with rust-colored hair,
reveals her mother has died three days ago
and that she has survived a short-order romance
with a man who gave her only a twenty-five-cent tip.
She brings us eggs, fried hard, one coffee,
one hot chocolate, toast with extra pads of butter.
It is early evening, but we sometimes like breakfast
food for dinner. My nine-year-old stomach growls
like a rabid canine. Sheila, the waitress, continues
to stand at our table as if we have magic to save her
from spending one more day in this diner.
Newly divorced, Mom shares the short version of abuse
we have endured from my dad, that our trip celebrates
our break from brutality. Sheila sympathizes, returns
to the counter.

Back in the motel, I slump onto my bed, soft
as a fresh donut, study ceiling, wonder
if half the world has lain on this mattress.

Next morning, we watch five hours of I-95 guide us
farther south. I lean my head against a window
filled with sunlight, slightly dizzy from the rush
of flatland scenery.

It's 6:00 p.m. when we drive down Magnolia Street,
an hour too late to visit the Fountain of Youth
and drink potion that promises to keep me
young forever.

LOSS I KNOW BY HEART

It was 1958. I was seventeen, drunk
for the first time. You were twenty-seven,
infatuated with my youth, had invited me
to a New Year's Eve party at your house.
Your wife was kind, seemed to accept
your feelings for me.

We had met when I interned as an apprentice
at a summer theater. You supervised me.
Since then, we had taken drives together
for several outings.

Many executives, from a television station
where you worked, gripped wine glasses,
exchanged workplace gossip. I leaned
against the fireplace, dizzy, unsteady.
You guided me to the basement door,
arm around my waist to keep me from falling
down steps, pungent smoke from the fireplace
stitched into your blue shirt. Beneath
a bare bulb in a porcelain fixture, I folded
to my knees, vomited. You held my forehead,
gave me physical comfort I would not allow
otherwise, insisted I stay the night.

Managing me to the bedroom, you removed
my clothes, helped me onto the bed. All night,
you slumped on a chair beside me, touched only
my hair to keep it off my damp forehead.

Semi-conscious, I heard you ask if
your nearness bothered me. I kept eyes closed,
didn't answer. I let you believe I slept,
both of us safe in ambiguity. Twice
before twilight, you addressed me
in a shallow whisper that sounded as far away
as snow outside. I didn't yet understand your way
of loving me was to call my name. Yours
was an impeccable restraint
to offset longing.

Next morning, I heard eggs break downstairs.
Your wife slouched across the table from me,
oblivious.

After breakfast, you drove me home, glanced
probably to see if I had grown wings to fly away
to keep merciless distance between us.
You asked how I felt about you. I coughed
into my hand, changed the subject.
Your face looked stricken as if you held me
responsible for icy surface beneath the car
that made driving treacherous. You parked
in my driveway. I got out. You didn't say
another word to me the rest of your life.

THE UNAVOIDABLE INTIMACY OF TEACHING

Even though it's a class of high school seniors,
I believe they can benefit from a lesson
in cursive writing, so I take time
from prescribed curriculum to instruct on
how to hold a pencil and slant paper
for the best result. I realize each student already
has established writing habits, but I feel a few tips
can make a difference.

As the class begins to practice
some of my suggestions, I amble around
the room, peer over each student's shoulder.
In row three, I stop at Joshua Reynolds' desk,
see that with a slight adjustment to paper's angle,
he will have perfect writing. I stoop close
to him as if we were starting love, but
there is no second-guessing as there would be
on the firing line of that emotion.
Up close, we handle each other easily.
Soap smell exudes from beneath his shirt collar.
I inhale his scent from the drunken air,
turn his paper slightly left. He seems amazed
a slight move could make so much difference.
Both of us satisfied, I pat him on the shoulder,
unbend from such delicate instruction.

RUMINATIONS DURING A TEACHER'S MEETING

The scent of mildewed carpet affronts me
as I open the library door, plop onto a chair.
I look around at worn faces, slumped bodies.
They look dangerously tired, defeated.
Eyelids droop. Seams of how we are put together
visible beneath fluorescence.

I think of escape, have a sweaty need to be
excused, to stand outside on school grounds
away from rotting carpet, predictable propaganda.
The system feels like a gigantic piranha
that threatens to swallow me in one flawless gulp.

I look at the sameness of everyone here,
begin to care that no one is unique. It frightens me
to be part of the monotony of this group and not
the exception. I close my eyes, hear frenzy
of motion, millions of restless particles of flesh
creating poses of attention.

The principal, an illusion of leadership, appears
to hate the least hint of intimacy.
He looks past a person, his eyes shift away,
refocus in an opposite direction.
He clears his throat, signal to begin,
a characteristic he confuses with dignity.
A pink tongue flicks from between fleshy jowls.

He empties a mouthful of language
toward blank faces. It appears as if we refuse
to assign meanings to his words. He goes on,
nevertheless, in a stuffy room, fur-lined,
claustrophobic.

I scan backs of balding heads, dyed hair,
mushy jawlines. I long to see the perfect
profile that can come out of this profession
like a lover after lovemaking, refreshed,
radiant, tinged with sublime difference.
It is sad in this room to witness omnipresent
fatigue, our retreat from autonomy, the way
we have strayed away from our own lives.

ARRIVING IN VENICE, ITALY, 1970

The Orient Express pulls into the Stanizone
di Venezia Santa Lucia at midnight. I descend
steps from the station to the Grand Canal.
Since I have no pre-arrangements for lodging,
I stroll along the calli, hope for a vacancy in a hotel.
It's 1:00 a.m. when I settle into my room
in the Hotel Canal Grande Venezia.

Excited to be in Venice, in spite of the late hour,
I stroll back to the walkway along the canal,
pass a few hustlers loitering in dim doorways.
I head toward the Bridge of Sighs which is not open
now, turn and start back toward the hotel.
A blunt moon and scratches of starlight scar black,
canal water. Streets are mostly vacant, seem sad
without people promenading. A young girl leans
against the front of a brick building, gives lipstick
a touch-up. A tall man in t-shirt and shorts lingers
on the winning side of hello, negotiates with her.

I re-enter the hotel, still expecting to pass through
portieres as if it were an opium den during old days
in Shanghai. Tomorrow, I will visit the Doge's Palace,
walk across the Bridge of Sighs, lunch at La Palanca.
Tomorrow night, I will investigate streets
of San Polo and Santa Croce, wend to where
streetlight dissolves in dead ends and shadowy
people come out before moonlight decays.

BUYING SOMETHING OLD

I used to drive in the country on Sunday
looking for antique shops or farms
that had antiques for sale. Anything buried
in time seemed valuable. I dressed in t-shirt,
jeans, drove my brown, Ford Capri on rural
roads until I spotted an empty barn. I hoped
my outfit suited country taste. More often
than not, I responded to newspaper ads
that promised a wealth of antiques relegated
to barns and of no longer any use to owners.

Sometimes, I encountered bargains:
$75 for a walnut bed the headboard of which
almost touched the ceiling, $5 for a gold-leaf
picture frame, $10 for a gilt-frame mirror.
I did most of this scrounging around for bargains
in the 1960s.

At one point, I lived by myself in German Village,
furnished my apartment with the walnut bed,
picture frame, and mirror. The only other thing
I could afford was a light bulb on a pole found
at Goodwill.

One Sunday afternoon, I followed an ad to a barn
in Pickaway County. I parked on a gravel driveway.
A woman, I estimated to be in her 60s, met me
at my car, led me to the barn where I found
another picture frame dramatically preserved

in the midst of spiraling dust and sunlight.
She didn't remember its origin, confessed
not appreciating it anymore. We chatted for a while
about the difference between modern furniture
and the old stuff. She preferred a little of both.

Driving twenty-six miles back to the Village,
I reminisced about my growing amount
of period pieces, decided the collection was
a metaphor for past time, my cavorting around
the country, an adventure not unlike Don Quixote's.
I was living life as passionately as I could,
collecting the past as if it could be purchased.

WHY A PUBLIC BEACH IS A PLACE FOR SELF-PITY

At a distance, multi-colored cabanas,
umbrellas, and folding chairs appear
as if a giant version of Joseph's coat
of many colors has been spread over
sand. I'm lying on a blue and white,
striped beach towel, rise on my elbows
in time to see a tan, young man step
from the changing cabana. He's
handsome as an old-fashioned movie star,
wears a turquoise swimsuit with white,
geometric designs. His has the kind
of looks and physique that an onlooker
stares at which is what I find myself doing.
Another fellow, equally attractive,
intercepts him. They saunter toward
a volleyball net, begin a doubles match.
They play no more than fifty feet from me,
and I think how I'm probably more
than fifty years older than they are, old
enough to be their grandparent.

Sun glints like a polished coin. I shade
my eyes, hide gawking and intimidation
behind Foster Grant sunglasses.
Their sweaty torsos catch light, look as if
they've been sprinkled with transparent glitter.
They exude an aura that suggests more
than friendship.

I look away, ego bruised, self-confidence sliced
like a knife wound. For a moment, I feel
as if I've taken a backseat in life.

I stand, fold my towel, trudge to my car,
the only passenger on a solitary ride home.

ASSORTED DESIRES WHILE WALKING ON NEWPORT STATE BEACH, CALIFORNIA

I amble along the tide line, see stars
connect to water. Their inextinguishable burn
anchored to the ocean's surface. Avarice enters
my mind, greed to keep this balmy, July night
in my back pocket to retrieve at home in Columbus,
Ohio when snow forces me to stay inside my house.

Tonight, a sultry breeze caresses,
warm as another human against my chest.
An old sky forces out milky light of the moon,
focuses a path on the sand that I follow toward the pier.
Sometimes, I stop, gaze at ocean's constant motion,
its vast expanse where unfortunate people get lost.
I inhale smell of seaweed which could be the breath
of sailors who have tasted terror of deep-sea death.
In any case, my lips savor tang of salt, moisten
from whiskey-drunk sensation of night's sweet air.

I'm a little exhausted from my walk, but before I turn
from this vast space to my rented cabin,
I press for the answer to a big question: What becomes
of a man dazzled by desire but of no consequence to anyone?
The question sizzles, crackles in my mind like a beach fire
I spot in the distance. As I near the blaze,
I see two men touch, a moment I will remember
like an unobtainable, envious gift.

THE LANGUAGE OF ICE

Along Alum Creek, tree limbs sag with snow
white as the old-fashioned habit of nuns.

I park my 1964 Oldsmobile, open the door,
shift on the seat so legs hang out,

slip feet into skates, lace them tight.
"California Dreaming" streams from the radio.

It's starting to snow again. Flakes, miniature
egrets, fly against the windshield.

Frozen creek holds my weight. I bend
at the waist, pump arms into motion, glide

forward, scribble lines on ice. Branches
on either side of the creek form

a glittering hallway, a nave in a cathedral.
For a brief time, I know solitude,

skim over infinite smoothness.
I am in a country made of water

that stands as still as a secret, etching
my signature on the cold

edges of December landscape.

BURNED AT THE CREATIVE STAKE

The atomic clock collects hours,
clock's tick the only sound in the house.

Acceleration of a distant car, drift of rust
to the bottom of the hot-water tank exist

only as half sounds. I slump at my desk.
It's 11:45 p.m. I look down at the first draft

of this poem, polish my glasses, push
the poem away, pull the chain on the

student lamp that illuminates imperfect words.
Does it come to a waste of time?

Other people mow a lawn, change a tire,
look for a miraculous cure for illnesses

while I dupe myself into thinking writing is more
important than anything else. At this point, I have

doubts. I feel I have squandered my life
in a word dance with a losing partner.

THE PERSUASION OF INK

I'm hunched over my desk, listening for truth,
its faintest sound the sound of breath. I reach
inside myself for what is innermost.
It could be God or my own spirit struggling
for existence on paper.

From a window above my desk, I inhale spring,
the aroma of newly mowed grass, hear traffic
rumble down Frebis Avenue. Though it is not night,
I switch on a student lamp. A circle of light
illuminates the legal pad. My eyes droop, feel old

as I try to reach inward for images: a cracked highway,
bakery heat of summer, windows early dark
with winter. I nudge my pen forward one line at a time,
enticement to finish as seductive as the smell
of fresh bread.

I stop for a moment, look away, think about an ending.
I scribble the last line as if it were an answer
to the big question of how to conclude a poem. Finished
as youth, the first draft yields a caress of accomplishment,

holds me closer than love in its satisfying embrace.

GLASS KNIVES

Glass knives do not make harmless slashes.
The only difference between a glass knife
and a chef's knife is transparency.

Any knife can empty a heart of blood,
but a glass knife leaves a person breathing,
eyes pointed to the ceiling, a hell of a gash

in a relationship. I have such a knife
lying atop the ink blotter on my desk.
I use it as a letter opener or a weapon

to cut truth from your heroin addiction.
You remember the gash I made in your life,
the blood-blue opening to truth to find

the reason for your long sojourns into dark
alleys. You showed me the boogie
of bad men, dealers who followed you

for payment. One particular night
you attempted to grab the knife from me.
We grappled, amateur gladiators,

grips white with anger to wield the weapon.
I twisted it from your fingers. You cried,
had planned to slice away lies, infidelity.

Next day, I replaced the knife on the desk.
Naked sunlight suffused the glass,
the unquestionable use of it to kill deception.

AMATEUR LOVE IN A BACK-ALLEY BAR

With an ache to become part of Friday
night's social rhythm, I saunter through
the door of Pigeonhole. Faces turn
in my direction, the obligatory, five-second
evaluation. I slide onto the only empty stool,
order Jack and Coke. Middle-aged men
swallow their drinks, steal glimpses
of themselves in the mirror behind
liquor bottles. The young dominate
the dance floor, gyrate to Purple Disco
Machine's "Substitution." Their arms reach
for the ceiling, heads thrown back
in euphoric oblivion.

The man sitting to my right asks
if he can buy me a drink. His thick, brown hair,
matching beard make him almost handsome.
His smile beguiles me. I accept the drink,
we exchange basic information, personal
stories. Eventually, he excuses himself
for a smoke on the patio. I can see him
out there from where I sit. He poses behind
lightning-bug-size glow of his cigarette.
When I look again, there is only space
where he stood. I long for his return,
for his company.

Peeking at the mirror, I see idle sulk
of lonely eyes that don't exactly know what

they're looking for. He won't come back.
He made his appropriate gesture, but
I didn't respond soon enough. I hear clamor
of regret in my head. Hesitation and timidity
canceled the possibility of a one-night stand
or a lifelong relationship. I slip off the stool,
sway toward the door, one drink too many.
My car is parked where a vapor lamp emits
flawed radiance.

NEW YEAR'S EVE AT THE COUNTRY CLUB

Light from Isabella's Crown, crystal chandeliers
brightens tuxedos and floor-length gowns.
Champagne flutes overflow with celebration.
My partner and I shuffle a dance, neck to neck.
A few couples leave early, their Limousines,
Mercedes streaking night with taillights red
as a painted fingernail or the bloodshot stare
of someone in purgatory. I see all of this,
as well as a blizzard, through floor to ceiling
windows. We are two hours from midnight,
half drunk, absurdly happy to be absurdly happy.

We gravitate to the bar, wear paper hats
that make us look like unemployed clowns.
I'm aware of fuzz in my brain, an assist in helping
to forget some of my life's failures. Clock hands
inch upward. Bartenders pace back and forth
in front of and behind each other, deliver
impersonality and disinterest along with drinks.
We grasp our glasses, edge away from the bar's
indifference, re-enter the dance area.

This time we waltz, one of my hands
on your waist, the other behind my back. You laugh
at my formal stance, and I tell you a gentleman
always knows how to pose for the occasion.
I shall never forget how within reach you are
at this moment during the last hour of the year.

The crowd swirls into the next dance, glistens
like assorted gemstones. Thereafter, clock
hands point to twelve, and the band segues
to "Auld Lang Syne." Commotion surrounds us.
We hug, kiss, clink a toast, wish each other the best.
Salutes to a new year dissolve as quickly as snowflakes,
and I am left with the thought we are no more than
a tearful blink of eternity's eyes, the momentary illusion
of happiness and promise now as finished as confetti
fallen across the ballroom floor.

PART TWO

THE EXTRAORDINARY SACRIFICE OF AUTUMN

Blood-red maple leaves quiver down
from a half-sun sky. I slouch to mailbox,
inhale slow breaths of mid-October air.
Heart failure and old age compel me
to take my time. Along the way, I note
landscape shutting down as if to sleep
through winter, leaves twisting off limbs,
stumbling across driveway from a push
of breeze. It's a season during which
I cannot ignore the absolutes of death,
the amazing spectacle of color tinged
with frost. I love these October days
as much as I loved green on green
of summer.

Yesterday, I unscrewed hoses from outside
spigots, replaced garden tools onto garage
brackets, cut final Queen Elizabeth roses
along the fence, brought the bouquet inside,
placed it in a cut-glass vase, a scrap of beauty
obtained from the cold.

Today, I practice acceptance of a fading season
that harbingers the hard hold winter will have
on me, of the howl of wolves deep in the woods,
sleeping close to their pack mates for warmth
while I sleep alone.

AUTUMN ELEGY

A maple leaf drops, a prophecy
of the downward rhythm of trees.

There is an essential pattern to dying,
a law that governs the moon,

recurrence of motion, heartbeats.
It is the same rhythm woodsmen use

to split wood and the oarsmen to row
their boats. Brittle sunlight assails leaves

the size of hands. Bent knuckles of oak,
clawing fingers of elm combust in fiery

colors. The name of winter lurks
like a dark word where white fences

encircle roadside markets, where
people purchase pumpkins and

gold-colored cider. It's the season
of sapphire sky, the season of smoke

from a bonfire of sparks near
a distant farmhouse. Snow buntings,

cardinals, dark-eyed juncos forgo
the miracle of migration, ignore

earth's magnetic pull, their silhouettes
outlined by shifts in shadows and winds.

FLOWER MOON

Moon, a circle of milk on black sky,
overflows with light that drips
from branches of the giant oak
in my front yard. I didn't remember
to retrieve mail earlier in the day, so
I walk a hundred-foot driveway
to the rural box. On my way back,
I stop, feel the moon's spectral presence
on my shoulders. It comes down
to a cliché about its light stirring
the blood, but its secondhand
illumination actually does something
invisible to the psyche. I wait
for a while, return its gaze, wonder
about eight billion people on the earth
who have pre-owned its influence.
No matter how long I stare, I still don't
know why it mangles my emotions,
makes me want someone or something
as out of reach as Uranus. It's an almost
palpable night. If I opened my mouth
wide enough, I could swallow stars.
It's a night when losses come back to haunt.

Reluctant to return to the house, to leave
this song of darkness, I allow aches and hurts
of the heart to resurface like vague phantoms.
People on this sixteen-house road are mostly
asleep. A neighbor's dog barks at an empty yard,

it's persistence never-ending. My throat still
wants to speak the ineffable, to articulate why
such luminescence incites lust. Instead, I shiver
off midnight's blameless caress, return to the house
before the moon burns it down.

A MARSH HAWK LEAVES THE PLANET ON A NOVEMBER NIGHT

As if greedy for flight, the Marsh Hawk gouges
pink ribbons of diminishing twilight, imprints
a path to the west, fades to disappearance.

I look after it, sight attached to nothing
but early night. I wrap my neck scarf tighter,
jamb hands deeper into warm pockets, start home

from Palm Pond. In the open field, I tromp
over corn stubble, look up at mica stars, small,
white windows in an infinite universe.

If only I had the means and grace to follow
that bird away from my solitary life, I would live
in sociable amazement. I think about the Marsh

Hawk wearing a flourish of infinity on its tail
feathers, transcending its habitat of sky, climbing
away from dark and desolation.

GEOMETRICS OF A SNOWY DAY

I don't remember sunlight, only snow
shutting down the city for three days.
I slip on boots, coat, knit hat, fur lined
gloves, grab a shovel from the garage.
Everything outside is blanketed in white
serenity. It takes imagination to identify
well-known objects: a porch, mailbox,
driveway, sidewalk. It seems as if what
is beneath these chalky mounds is myth,
unknown. Yesterday, I built hills to the
height of wings. Today, I shovel a new
accumulation against mocking wind.
An icy layer sheaths snow deep as doubt.
Ice won't scoop, so I use the shovel like
a blade to crack frozen surface. It is 22°
Fahrenheit, cold as estranged love.
Not even a hint of blunted sun shows
behind gray sky. It's a colorless day.

My shovel cracks ice, and I see sidewalk,
trowel marks in cement, breadcrumbs
dropped for birds before bad weather. I
unbend for a break, gaze at backyard white
as the muzzle of an old dog. Another snow
squall is predicted for later today. A riot
of flakes will obscure all that I've cleared,
and I'll start again, maybe finish at night
by flood light. I trudge to the garage,
slip off my boots, turn my back on
a moon-colored world I hardly recognize.

DO BIRDS IN OHIO SING IN THE WINTER?

In dreams, I've been a Confederate soldier,
legionnaire, John Keats, Edgar Allan Poe,
the Crown Prince of Saudi Arabia, believing
myself to be as important as a Bartok concerto,
and, in those dreams, words smeared across my sleep
like smudged tire tracks on a snowy road,
words that said you're not very handsome.

It is winter when these dreams occur,
and I awaken in the middle of the night, look
out the window at tree limbs which appear black
laces on a boot of night.

Yesterday, I pointed a stick at a worm on a leaf,
flipped the worm into oblivion. A loss? A freedom?
It is not as cataclysmic as my own disappearance
into bizarre and unfulfilling dreams.

Again, I sleep, dream, become fog, try to paint
myself back into existence: eyes, nose, a face begin
to form on canvas. I stare at the emerging portrait,
exasperated with results, smash the brush against pastels,
pinks, cadmium reds, pain in my hand sharper
than the cut of a palette knife.

I blink awake. White-throated sparrows sing
like morning saints at prayer, intoxication
after unpeaceful dreams, an elixir to eliminate
remaining thistles in my brain.

SNOW AS DENOUEMENT

It's late afternoon, and snow has powdered down
since early this morning. This much accumulation
makes a difference in the way people regard the world
as a better place, a milky landscape that has erased
the mundane.

When I look out the window, I think I see
same snowflakes I remember from childhood. If so,
they keep coming back like my own possessions
keep coming back newly wrapped as gifts
on my April-fool birthday.

Power lines sag. Streets turn white as if scribbled on
by a gigantic piece of chalk. Drivers slow down
to a funeral-procession pace. Buildings become colorless
like bed sheets over stored furniture.

A pessimist might say the day is ruined
when the first flake falls, but I like the illusion
of immaculateness brought to earth by dark, gray clouds,
purity akin to innocence.

Burst of flame in the fireplace shines against chill.
Again, I look out the window, watch sky continue
to spew snow, find it impossible to see separation
between heaven and horizon, happiness and
excessive melancholy.

LEAVES

I understand leaves. Their serrated tongues
wag intense talk of death in whirls of October

wind. A gust of pre-winter stirs a cluster
of maple leaves, curls them upward for seconds

of false resurrection. Not all leaves come down
with the blush of defeat. Some stay attached

like an ambiguous defiance of demise.
Crows coast overhead, grating coos, caws, rattles,

and clicks escaping their throats. Most of what
grows green disappears like divas in a final,

seasonal bow. On either side of rural roads,
color, as audacious as the first days of spring,

rains down on forest foliage. Autumn, the showiest
of seasons, brims like an overnight rainbow.

It's an adagio of audacious red, orange, and yellow.
It's a whirling, gyrating, chromatic caper .

Air is the ballroom filled with spinning, twirling
leaves, dead at the end of the dance.

PART THREE

LITCHFIELD BEACH, SOUTH CAROLINA

She spreads sunscreen over turnip-white skin,
watches college students splash through surf
to deeper water where they dip and bob
like human corks. She leans back in her folding
chair, can't seem to look away from the bathers.

She's traveled with fellow teachers from Ohio
to enjoy spring break near the ocean, but,
as usual, in spite of friends, she feels lonely
as the last Baiji Dolphin.

She gazes at the frisky, young men frolicking
with each other in the water, wishes she could
be years younger than fifty-three and cavort
with them. In truth, she desires to satisfy
latent passion, to touch their youth not only
with her eyes but with her very hands.

She continues to slip looks to the boys
who have sprawled on beach towels, letting
sun dry water drops that sparkle on their skin
like transparent sequins. She knows there is
no way out of the hell of being older, of the pain
of wanting to be part of a younger generation.
She answers herself with a mental slap
for having such foolish urges, moments that stain
reason with blind lust.

She folds her chair, feels like a weed in a garden
of youthful flesh, slogs back to the rented house
and to predictable routines of people her own age.

STUD

He didn't choose to be born
with the blackest beard on the block,
yet, it seems he did get born with a strut.
Ass, a perfect distance from ground,
moves with balanced rhythm,
girlfriend in tow beside him, an advertisement
for all is well in my world. When he precedes
you in a crowd, your scarecrow reflection
in a storefront window seems even more
ragged. Pomaded hair, long on the neck,
placed carelessly perfect, glistens
like old- fashioned snake oil. You want
to look hard at him, ask if he catches on
to how he exists for the nondescript majority
who leave enough room around him for awe.
Is it a matter of illusion that he suffers
no human afflictions such as dirty fingernails
and death? He is lucky all right.
The world strokes him, nuzzles up
to his nonsense, undresses for him on cue.
He's the whole tree, and you, the underside
of one of his leaves.

You've been accused that this is a flimsy way
to think. "You ought to be ashamed
of wanting to be other than who you are."
You've been admonished to accept paltry genes.
You howl at unfairness, curse indiscriminate heredity.

He ambles across shopping-center, parking lot,
beautiful bones mere shadows beneath his skin.
You start your car, inch toward the traffic signal,
watch him in the rear-view mirror, his essence
ready to kindle envy in someone else's conversation.

HE'LL MAKE ANOTHER DOLLAR

He unbuttons the top button of her Prada sheer,
organza, pleated blouse, and the next button
and the next, unfastens her Bottega jeans.
Light from a single candle pours over
the fifty-six-year-old profile of her nakedness
and the male escort she has employed. Tonight,
she affords Eli's $500-an-hour fee. At sixteen,
her husband bought his first stocks, invested
the profit in real estate. High yields from land
investments resulted in a net worth of ten million.
He settles at home less and less, claims after-hour
business demands his attention. Their marriage
is tenuous. He traded intimacy for a small fortune.

When Eli was fifteen, a lifeguard at Crystal Pool,
his green eyes and ripped physique attracted female
groupies. He quickly learned dynamics of sexually
manipulating interested young ladies. Now,
a nineteen-year-old Lothario, he services
this neglected wife for the second time in a week.

They clasp each other, edge to the bed.
She wraps her arms around his neck as if he were
the infinite answer to loneliness. Their love making
is mechanical, a paid-for routine. Never does either
ask the other why they empty their lives
into each other's vacuous presence.

He is satisfied beyond doubt with the envelope
of cash she left for him on the kitchen counter.
She accepts his detached body as readily as she would
a glass of wine, knows he's there only for the money
and not for her ultimate fulfillment. She sees him
to the door, his work finished, her satisfaction temporary.

HUSTLER'S SPORT

You didn't leave the gay bar with the man
you shared drinks with and talked to
for over an hour, a handsome man in his 20s,
closed-cropped, brown hair, depthless, green eyes
you couldn't see what intent lay at the bottom of.
He hadn't said anything or made any moves
to suggest sexual interest.

Outside, however, you found him loitering
under a streetlamp. He nodded. You sensed
his signal to follow, and you did. Side by side,
you dawdled down an alley between ramshackled
buildings toward the parking lot. His quick
movements slid a pocket knife from your neck
to your navel as if he were a slaughterhouse butcher.
Blood, the color of a tropical sunset, gushed out of you,
mixed with brown leaves, cigarette butts, beer cans.
Your eyes glossed open past possibility of seeing
starlight reveal your insides.

Morning news didn't mention the LGBTQ murder,
the hustler, or his new acquaintance. It didn't happen
in this Bible-thumping, midwestern city clean
as a white sheet over an autopsy.

PASSION OFF THE STREET, 1970

Kai passes the afternoon in an adult theater,
lounges on red, carpeted steps leading
to the projection room. Men cruise each other
in the lobby, parade back and forth, hungry hunters.
A good-looking, young man perches on the step
beside Kai. He introduces himself as Colter.
Though it is semi-dark on the stairs, Kai is attracted
to the man's close cropped, brown hair, hazel eyes.
Colter's sadness bleeds from his face like a facial dirge.
Both men wear Levi's, white t-shirts, a thinly disguised urge
to connect. Colter fumbles a small bottle, the color of
tobacco juice, from his pocket, hands it to Kai,
says, "Sniff it." Kai uncaps the bottle, inhales.
His brain melts. He sees cloudless sky, bright as a burning
cigarette, come as close to his face as a kiss.
He recaps the bottle with a genie inside.
Colter takes it back like a selfish Aladdin. Kai rises
to leave, ambles down the aisle toward flashes
from the movie screen, plans to exit out the back door
to the alley adjacent to the parking lot, but
when he pulls back the frayed, maroon curtain
leading to the exit, two men are standing in near darkness,
pants around ankles. One of them puts a hand on Kai's
shoulder to stop movement. It is an unsafe place
for the man's mouth to desire Kai's body.
In seconds, the stranger takes from Kai the taste
of carnal fate, fulfillment Kai will be looking for
the rest of his life.

NIGHT PRIVILEGES

Chad strolls along a canal in De Wallen,
the largest red-light district in Amsterdam.
His eyes flirt from one prostitute to another,
ladies who wait in rented, one-room cabins.
They offer services from behind a window
or a glass door illuminated by light red
as the devil's bloodshot eye. Occasionally,
Chad glances at the canal, dark and murky
like doubt about what his next move will be.

People pack the street. It's Mardi Gras
along a canal. Atmosphere hums with
sexual enticement. Chad stops in front of
a window. A girl with blonde hair smiles
at him, enough cleavage revealed to lure
a monk. Her blue bikini is more a suggestion
than a garment.

She opens the glass door, and he enters
past red light. Chad offers her thirty euros
for twenty minutes. With a thick Dutch
accent she introduces herself as Emma,
takes him by the hand, leads him to bed.

He feels her heart thump against his chest,
sucks in purchased warmth of her mouth,
grinds deep into desire, opens her anticipation,
drives home his intent.

Subsequently, they re-dress, and she unbolts
the door for him to leave. He stands outside
for a minute, looks at her through the red-lit window.
She doesn't look at him. Her eyes already focused
on yet another stranger, someone else ready
to spend thirty euros on momentary satisfaction
of conveyor-belt ecstasy.

SAILBOAT ARRANGEMENT

We launch the Sunfish from the beach,
jump onto the board-like hull. Muscle-knotted,
sweat-slick tightness of your arms man
the Oceanic lateen sail. At first, the sail falters,
then an upwind catches its polyester slack,
strengthens our aimless destination
on the reservoir. Sun, bright as an arc lamp,
boils our bodies. Even wearing sunglasses,
we squint to see the bow cut water.

Ahead, horizon, like skyline's hem, flickers
a silver washout of light. We follow
no particular path, remove t-shirts, relax
into camaraderie. We are temporary sailors,
naming boat parts, letting our closeness count
as unspoken affection, but less than fidelity
of the flesh. We agree sailing is a dizzying
narcotic, a disappearance into euphoric escape.

Tacking toward the end of the sky, my throat
swells with urge to tell you it is not wrong for us,
but you are married to a wife who winds herself
around you whenever in someone else's presence.

My mind takes a sharp turn away from my tongue.
I remain silent, stare as you handle the rigging,
accept that we have no set direction.
We, and the ghost of possibility, continue to cut
through corridors of sunlight and sparkling spray.

UNBEARABLE AND FIERCE MERCY IN THE BOOKSTORE

His sweaty hand slips on the glossy book
cover as he focuses on her standing
behind the cashier's counter. He didn't notice
her when he first entered, but when
he removed a book from the shelf, turned back
toward the entrance, she became his desire.

His hand flips pages without looking.
Her creamy skin, gray eyes, brown hair with
auburn highlights enamor him. He replaces
the book, picks up another, opens it, his
concentration elsewhere. She doesn't notice
him staring at her.

He strolls to another shelf to avoid suspicion,
even though she is still visible. He leans
his head sideways to read titles, finger
skimming one binding after another.
If he were asked, he would admit quick
infatuation smacks of an adolescent crush,

a momentary obsession. He decides
to buy *The Craving Impulse*, a fiction book
with white cover, gold, embossed lettering.
He digs his wallet out, finds his place in line,
wishes he had shaved, prepared for the unforeseen.
Nervous, he motions for the person behind him

to move forward. Minutes later, he's at the checkout,
fumbles out a $20 bill. Except for words to transact
the sale, she says nothing. He slumps out of the shop
to his car, embarrassed by foolish feelings,
steers to the nearest McDonald's, breaks the spell of her
with a burger and fries.

SEXUAL SNOW

Like trillions of paint chips, snow peels
from sky, accumulates, colors landscape
white as altar cloth.

Emma watches the squall from the living room
window. Childless, she imagines the snow falls
into her barrenness.

The mailman, practically obliterated by hazy air,
delivers letters she no longer cares about, jottings
from a man who claimed he loved her, stole money

as well as serenity. She opens the front door,
retrieves junk mail, rips it in half. Snow dust whirls
from porch railing in an upsweep of wind.

She wants the beauty of snow to overflow her womb,
freeze her from feeling motherless. Inside,
she collapses into a club chair, watches logs blaze

in the fireplace, has only a sour memory
of making love to a man who lay frigid in her bed,
who ended up wanting other men.

There is nothing between her legs
but billowing vacancy of virtue. She dozes,
firelight warming her face,

snow in her maidenhead never melting.

WASTED SEX

It takes marijuana for you to want intimacy.
Otherwise, I have to horsewhip you into bed.
Sometimes, it almost comes down to that.
There is no song in your head about love.
Our body closeness feels more like an accident
than intentional.

You slip out of your clothes, flop onto the bed,
lie there like a mummy waiting to be wrapped
in linen, legs tightly together, unyielding.
I follow your breathing, watch inhalation,
exhalation, hoping it is a preamble to erotic affinity.

We're in a darkened room. A bit of light
from a vapor lamp outside the window slants
across us, etches you in shadow which is
how I feel about your presence. It wouldn't surprise,
when I finally touch you, if my fingers slide through
your invisibility to the mattress. Even
with you beside me, the bed feels empty.

I can't name emotion that seeps from impatience.
I wait for the burn of anger, push it aside, relent,
put my fingers around your frigidity. You succumb,
allow me a one-man show, and then you go limp.

Afterward, you dress, prepare to leave.
I conclude I would have been more gratified
by self-stimulation than by trying to coax you
out of indifference and a self-induced, drug coma.

Ready to go, you throw me a goodbye,
a baseball full of nothing I catch
with my bare hand.

TACK ROOM

A cloudburst causes them to canter back
to the tack room. Eleanor and Riley, lovers,

dismount Morgan horses among saddles,
bridles, stirrups, and reigns. He brushes

wet hair from his forehead. She towel-dries
her face. They slip out of damp clothes.

Fists of rain hammer tin roof, motivate them
to embrace each other's nakedness

on a saddle blanket. He hugs her to his chest,
breathless to touch every inch of her immaculate

skin, wraps her in silent warmth, presses into
the triangle of her ready acceptance.

On the other side of satisfaction, they lie silent
as a painting, listen to rain diminish to

an almost inaudible drizzle. It is blue-black outside
the windows. Inside, there is just enough light

for them to see each other's contours, to see
themselves pull together again and again

to answer a need that keeps resurfacing
like persistent passion.

COMFORTABLE DOUBT

I unfold a card table in the living room,
heft sewing machine onto it, aim thread
through the needle's eye. My husband
and I lounge near the fireplace, lathered
in firelight. He chugs a beer behind an
issue of *Sports Illustrated.* Lives are
short, questions, necessary, but he has
never asked why I let time ooze through
my sewing machine nine stitches per inch.

I think I succeeded at this marriage,
stepped into predictable routines, fulfilled
marriage promises according to contract.
We have not yielded to outsiders
for sexual gladness no matter how gorgeous
the moment. I have wondered, occasionally,
why he hasn't slept with someone else.
For fifty years, we've adhered to rules
of commitment, fixed them into our lives
like photos pasted into an earlier album.

I slump across from him, gray haired,
a bit wrinkled. I slide cloth beneath the fang
of the needle, mend suit trousers, a shirt,
a favorite sweatshirt he calls "play clothes."
Thread unspools, pierces cloth I feed across
the metal plate hand over hand. His face
sweats from the glare of fire.

I grab another shirt from my work basket,
think how ordinary we have become.
What might have been only a hotel affair
spiraled into front-porch Sundays.
We used to lean against porch railing,
feeling small as two items in the local paper,
or we swayed in the swing to an unconscious
sexual rhythm. Now and then, he leaned
his head back, eyes brooding as if
I had denied him as a lover.

He clears his throat. Is this the moment
I find out there have been other Sunday people
in his life waiting in the jagged moonlight?
As the cliché says, "Some questions are better
left unanswered." Nobody knows
where I have been or where I am,
this minute or the next,
but him.

THE WET-GRASS MOON

A docile woman without dreams, devoid
of inclinations, desires consummately hidden,

strolls from her summer porch to the driveway,
stands as still as stars. It's past midnight, but

she can't sleep. Night seems to have invited her
outside to loll in July moonlight. It's uncommonly

cool. Grass glitters with dew. She fusses her
blue, pajama collar, an expert at guarding virginity

for sixty-three years. She looks at hedges in need
of trimming, lawn slightly overgrown. Fireflies,

yellow brooches, pin themselves to night's black coat.
If someone should step from shadows, ignore her

composure, bargain for her virtue, would she relent?
She would say *only after marriage* and tip her prim head

away. She's sways in a self-waltz with solitude,
dances with undauntable forbearance.

In an uninhibited second, she hugs her chest,
enfolds moonlight in both arms, a facsimile of love.

ESSENTIAL FROST

The night is as cold as an angel's face.
We drive gravel road from my aunt's cabin
on Big Darby Creek to the highway.
I have to get out, unlock a gate for us to pass.
Our day-long getaway has not resolved
the question of why we have become separate
from one another. You adjust the car's heater..
Our conversation becomes neutral. Clichés
give way to silence. You stare at dashboard
lights as if you see speed at which our journey
together has become joyless. You tell me
I must be kind to myself, that it's not my fault
our relationship didn't work, that we share
equal responsibility for the loss. My thoughts,
like a hot iron, press failure into fact.

As we drive, my mind collects evidence
of what we were once, breaks it down
into little pieces under the auspices of knowledge.
You tear open a cigarette pack, light up,
tip of the cigarette burning 900° Celsius,
a miniature sun.

I speak for the first time in twenty minutes.
You slump against the side window, reflection
a black stain shadowed in the glass. I brake
in front of your house where clots of weeds glitter
frost. You turn to me with no promise to stay
in touch, enter your house through a door
with a bedsheet over its window. I feel finished,
cast a last look at where I will never return.

A VULNERABLE CHOICE AT VERMILION, OHIO

We've rented a two-bedroom cabin on Lake Erie,
swam all day in sun-warm water. At dinner time,
we showered sand from our bodies, drove to Rudy's
Bar & Grill. You ordered boneless wings.
I requested crab cakes. We both swilled a couple
Budweisers. After dinner, we returned
to our separate rooms.

All day, the urge to touch you stirred desire
for more than friendship. From my room,
I watched across the hall as your clothes collapsed
to the floor, and you slid onto bedsheets.
You reached toward the nightstand, snapped off the lamp.
Unexpected moonlight sculpted your nakedness.
My face burned with embarrassment for peeping.
I imagined my cheeks red as Georgia clay.
What to do next? The answer blazed in my brain.
My mouth dry, I waited for my legs to move.
I crossed the hall, quiet as a shadow, knelt
at bedside close to your head, became part of the dark
matter in the space of your room. My arms encircled
you, my warm breath against yours. My head spun,
dizzy from being on the other side of the threshold.
You rolled onto your side, stared at me, said yes.

DUPED ON SANTIBEL ISLAND

Clouds, white as cauliflower, overflow
sky's edges above the Gulf of Mexico.
I lean on elbows atop a blue and green,
striped beach towel, gaze past sun's glare
at sunbathers and swimmers. Men with
sculpted pecs throw pitch-and-catch glances
at girls in skimpy bikinis. Babies spring
from restraining hands, plucked back
to safety by vigilant mothers. Old people
with bulging waists hide wrinkled eyes
behind sunglasses.

Maybe because of half-clad bodies, or
maybe because of relentless undulations
of water, sensuality exists on the beach
as omnipresent as sand. I rise, stretch,
amble toward a swim. I wade past surf,
dog paddle until I'm waist deep.
A young man next to me smiles hello.
I return the greeting. Water beads like wet
stars that sparkle on his blonde hair, suntanned
shoulders. Mutual desire buoys between us
as noticeable as sky. He asks if I have a cabin.
I answer yes. Even though I know such
minimal satisfaction is more dangerous than sun,
I agree to meet him at 4:00 p.m., hunger for hookup
as loose in my head as an escaped animal.

At 4:00, I perch on a large, ornamental rock
outside my door, wait for two hours.

He never appears. I trudge back to the beach.
He is not there. I fill with unbounded deception.
The experience leaves me empty, feeling foolish
as a court jester. Tonight, I will sing the song
of my mistake to the dark, regret I mistook him
for a better song.

JESUS FINALE

Blazing sunlight permeates a stained-glass image
of Jesus Christ above the sanctuary in the Church
of Christ. His robe alternates red and maroon panels.
His left hand holds a shepherd's staff, his right, a lamb.
A gold halo surrounds his head.

When Kanan was a month old, Reverend Richards
baptized Kanan in this church. Since then,
the sixteen-year-old has never missed a Sunday service,
attended Sunday school, took his first communion
when he was in the second grade. His parents are
inordinately proud of their only son. All is well
until a certain, pivotal Sunday.

Hymns had been sung, scripture read, and psalm 62
recited: "My soul waits for God alone..." Service
finished, parishioners disperse. Kanan hops into
the 1955 Oldsmobile his aunt gave him, drives home,
doffs dress pants, white shirt, tie, slips into Levi's
and t-shirt. It is 1:00 p.m. He promised
Reverend Richards to return at 3:00 to discuss
the church's summer, outreach program.
Kanan decides to leave early.

With no one present, the church is eerily quiet,
sacrosanct, inviolate. Reverend Richards has told Kanan
to come to the sacristy. Kanan doesn't think it matters
that he is an hour early. He thinks early arrival illustrates
enthusiasm for the program.

He doesn't knock but slowly turns the knob
on the closed door. It opens to reveal two nude people:
Reverend Richards and a boy Kanan knows to be
no more than fourteen. Flushed with embarrassment,
Kanan pivots back the way he came. His head brims
with conflicting emotions, but anger predominates.

Next day, at the same time, he returns to the church,
carries a bag of rocks. Again, the nave is quiet
as a mausoleum. He approaches the stained-glass
window, lifts a rock from the bag, pitches it as hard as he can.
The halo around Christ's head shatters as fast as Kanan's faith.
He continues to wing rocks at the window until
only a few shards are left. Disturbance brings Reverend
Richards from the sacristy. He simply stands and watches the
boy hurl exasperation at Jesus until nothing remains
but spiritual defeat and an empty, window frame.

PART FOUR

THE WRONG LANGUAGE

Her easy talk of snow refusing to be white,
frightened me. Even though I had become
used to the onslaught of Alzheimer's, now
and then, Aunt Liz's words startled me
into remembering how erratic, unreasonable,
and illogical her thoughts could be. I simply
smiled, wrapped an arm around her shoulder
and said yes.

She continued to stand at the living room window,
watching traffic and activity in the parking lot
of the Haviland Club bar across the street.
Sometimes, she raised ready binoculars
to get a close up of someone staggering to a car.
It was cheap entertainment that lasted until
2:00 a.m. Even from her recliner, she had
a clear view of prostitutes, police, and
drug transactions.

I had read about Alzheimer's in books, but
personal experience taught me, first hand,
how to behave with someone whose mind had been
sabotaged by the uncompromising disease.
I prayed for a genius to come up with a cure.

In the meantime, I applied her lipstick, shaped
eyebrows, roughed sunken cheeks, made certain
to be within view as much as possible.

It was a full-time job to keep her functional.
I no longer had time to myself.

The last year of my teaching career, I graded papers
on a table placed between her chair and mine.
That way, she could see that I had not been abducted
by the followers, mysterious people whom she said
constantly spied on us.

Once, we spent the afternoon sorting old
greeting cards. She didn't recognize names
of senders, only commented on the pretty
pictures and the number of people who had
remembered us. Next thing, when I looked
up, she was dozing, chin on chest as if
she didn't want to see any more of the past.

A STUDY OF AUNT LIZ'S FAILING HEALTH ONE FEBRUARY EVENING

She slumps asleep in her recliner.
Streetlight through the living room window

reveals ninety-five year-old neck folds accumulated
on her chest. I linger in the hall that separates us,

stare as if gazing will reveal the secret
of how she has defied death since

her Alzheimer's diagnosis. Her urge to stay alive
terrifies me because such resistance

can only last so long. Though her head drowses,
she demands life. I can see it in her careful breaths.

Earlier in the day, I applied rouge, eyebrow pencil,
lipstick, a mask to hide decrepitude, a disguise

she wears to sleep in blue, cotton pajamas,
dangerously relaxed toward more then rest.

BLOOD NOTES

If you have to die, do it without me.
I've seen too many family deaths
to witness another. These brutal thoughts
roll through my mind as I stand
in the hallway looking at Aunt Liz
slumped in her recliner in the living room.

She wears a blouse white as an honor guard's
gloves or pallbearer's. Blood spots saturate
the front of her blouse like smashed, red roses.
She has just spit blood into the kitchen sink.
Her late-night movement awakened me.

Still half asleep, I plod to her side, ask
if she is all right. I always keep a storage bag
of chopped ice in the freezer, and when
she begins to spit up blood, she eats the ice.
It tends to stop the flow.

The specialist diagnosed pulmonary fibrosis,
said hemorrhaging wouldn't kill her.
She fights fear that it will.

When I know she is calm, coughing stopped,
I return to bed, crawl into a fetal position,
feel free to sleep, but guilty to have left her alone.

I drop off thinking about the next time
she has an episode, how I will stand by her
at the sink while her crumbling lungs
are answered with ice.

OCCASIONAL STILL LIFE

Succumbed to sleep in her recliner,
Aunt Liz appears dead. As if
rigor mortis has set in, her head lulls
to one side like the broken neck
of a swan folded into itself.
From the other side, neck skin
has stretched into a younger face.
Her mouth, it's strength gone, hangs
open as if frozen into a steady scream.
A tissue has fallen out of her hand,
arm nearly draped to the floor.
She has become as inert as a piece
of furniture. I stand by her chair,
watch her chest for breathing,
drop into an opposite chair, study
her, a painting I am waiting
to come alive. To my right, cold
sunlight floods through a window.
Cedar limbs bounce in November
breeze. I rise from the wingback,
feel awkward to leave her alone,
believe she will only stay alive
while I hold her in my eyes, believe
strings tied to my feet will pull her
into death if I move away.

TOOLS

When my uncle Toots died, I moved in with his wife,
Aunt Liz. When she died, I inherited her house.
My uncle could fix anything, a jack-of-all-trades,
master of them all.

One autumn afternoon, when I was sweeping the basement,
I stopped in front of pegboard on which hung various
saws, ball-peen hammers, mallets, planes, curved-jaw pliers,
dozens of other tools I couldn't name.

During thirty-seven years I lived in this house, I had organized,
rearranged the tools many times. I did it
with my uncle's memory in mind. He liked neatness,
so I kept this part of my inheritance as tidy and
well-ordered as I could.

I still picture him at his workbench under fluorescent light,
constructing makeshift items from cast-off scraps.
He built a four-shelf, basement closet from the crate
in which a coal-burning furnace had been delivered.
He constructed his workbench from spare lumber,
made a wine cabinet from scrap wood. I, on the other hand,
do not possess an interest or skills to make use of these tools.
I am simply the custodian of implements.

He left no hint of how I could acquire his natural talent
or be as self-sufficient as he was. He never called
for a service. He did everything himself. Growing up
during the Depression, he depended on self-reliance.

A coppery glow from sunset splashes a window, and
I wonder, again, what he would want regarding the tools:
to sell them? keep them? learn to use them as effectively
as he did?

I climb basement steps away from questions,
away from possibility he may be judging me
from his place deep in the earth.

IN JUDGMENT OF THINGS

I am aware of nothing but details
in the living room: figurine lamps
with red, fringed, faded shades,
a floral carpet, petals worn from wear,
windows too small. It's a suffocating
room with an amassment of knick knacks
and too many tables. A mirror hangs
on every wall dwarfed by the large mirror
above the fireplace.

Aunt Ada's Max-Factor face boasts vanity.
Flame-red lipstick smeared across her mouth
twists into a perpetual sneer. She hasn't gone
to bed for two weeks, refuses to eat,
sustains herself on Keystone Light. Dementia,
like an unwanted winter tumor of ice
behind an automobile wheel, has turned her life
into a small cycle of bathroom visits and
alcohol consumption.

Her only son, a useless drunk, lives with
his latest floozy in an apartment a block away,
ignores his mother's condition and doesn't visit.
I have lived with her for ten years, the nephew
she adores who has now become a stranger.

I've sunk into a large, gray, sectional couch
that takes up one end of the room.
She has sagged into her recliner across from me.

I stare at her, and she stares at the TV, not really
watching it, unable to follow a narrative. I assume
one of her six sisters will soon step in,
arrange for hospitalization. One of them notified
the son who hasn't responded.

It seems, during the last fourteen days, I've watched her
grow old beyond eighty-six years. Though necessary,
I dread the day they'll take her away. Regardless
of the weather, she'll want to wear her imitation,
fox-fur coat and carry an extra lipstick in her blouse
pocket. I'm beginning to hate this room
where too much of everything persists, where
I seem to be watching the calm of her dying,
where objects are more permanent than life.

AUNT ADA

I push open the door to her room
where she is surrendering life,
perch on the edge of her bed.
She's been bedridden for a week.
I have lived with her for ten years,
moved in after her husband died
because she was afraid to live alone,
and I couldn't afford my rented
apartment any longer. Her only
grandson occupies a spare room
across the hall. I'm frightened
that she will be frightened, hate
my own breath for being useless.
I look around the room, remember
a collection of black dresses from
the 1940s, sleeve to sleeve in the closet.
Faded doilies on the Victrola top
would come apart if not handled carefully.
Seven antique lamps in the living room
burn dim as December sun.
When I was a kid, I stayed all night
whenever my uncle worked night shift
at the Federal Glass Company.
She would fix scrambled eggs, fried potatoes,
applesauce, and toast for breakfast.
I think of her as a woman living
in the kitchen, feeding anyone who stopped by
with homemade cooking. One summer,
she baked and froze forty apple pies.

I bragged about that. It showed domesticity
I associate only with the old days.
I ask if she's cold, slip out, turn up the thermostat.
Back in her room, I count clutter
of accumulated souvenirs that cover the dresser.
Pearl and plastic-handled hair brushes share space
with a half dozen brilliant, red, lipsticks.
I gaze at these things because I know
the grandson, smoking endless cigarettes, is already
deciding how to undecorate after her death.

DEVOTION

Uncle Heine fenced strawberries away
from rabbits, pampered rose bushes with peat
and patience, believed he could conjure
the perfect garden out of the earth. Audacious
blood of a farmer boiled in his veins.
He believed hard work would yield crops
the envy of family and neighbors. He toiled
from sunrise to suppertime, returned to the garden
after he ate, labored until light slipped
below the horizon like a last, communion wafer.

Spring and summer, he awakened with an amateur's
dream to see what he had coaxed from soil.
He recognized his connection to the ancient act
of cultivating, spaded hope, gazed happily at first
sprouts. Dragging a hose from the house, he sprayed
summer water over plants, seemed to wash sunshine
off the sky when he flipped the hose upward.

Hundreds of hours swept around the clock
away from sacred beginnings as plants ripened
to fruition. Hose water beaded onto tomato skins
the color of coxcomb. Sometimes, he would stand
at the edge of his garden, stare at his efforts.

Once, when I was visiting, I lingered near
rows of cabbage, and he said, "When you garden,
you must keep a balance between nurturing and trust,
and nothing you plant will see light without Love."

When Uncle Heine and his wife, Aunt Ada, died,
I inherited their estate. One spring afternoon, I loitered
in their garage, meaning to clean, but let myself, instead,
be wrapped in reminiscence. Sunlight overwhelmed
Uncle Heine's garden tools. Rake, hoe, shovels, plow
had rusted a little. What saddened me was not just
the torpor of these tools, but that someday,
at the beginning of a growing season, they would fall
into ungrateful and graceless hands.

RELUCTANCE

Mom and two of her sisters have grown old:
white-haired widows, blotched with age spots,
crinkled faces under dining room light as
they rise from the Thanksgiving table,
ears mostly without hearing, movement stiffened,
barely carrying them to the next chair.

In the living room, they slouch into Mackinaw-warmth
of overstuffed recliners, conversation a collection
of episodes they remember as a perfect childhood.
I think back to preparation for this dinner when
I watched Mom, Aunt Liz, and Aunt Ada slide
dinner rolls into the oven, scramble pots and pans
from one burner to another, infuse silence with clatter
of silverware as they arranged knives, spoons, forks
with merciless precision.

Now, late in the afternoon, they slump.
Russet reflections from the stone fireplace reveal
their fatigue . Occasionally, one of the women leaves
the room, returns with makeup freshly painted.
Mom and Aunt Liz are in their nineties, Aunt Ada
in late eighties. In spite of room's cozy security
and buzz of endless talk, imminence of death lounges
like an uninvited guest and a reminder of deceased
uncles.

These women depend on the habit of Thanksgiving
dinner as if it were a favorite cardigan

hung on the same hook to wear year after year.
They have assured each other that life is permanent,
believe the end will not happen, believe the shock
of graceless passing is not, for them,
a likely possibility.

A TALE OF AUNT CLARA

It always rained on our trips to Dayton
to see Aunt Clara, oldest of seven sisters.
On this particular day, sky closed a door
on light, shaded color from landscape.
Gray rolled by car windows for over an
hour until we reached Wilmington Pike
and the gravel driveway leading to a brick
farmhouse with grandiose porch, slate
roof, and an oak door with beveled, glass
panels that looked into a room in need
of flowers.

Aunt Clara met us before the first knock,
her welcome as honest as a legitimate banker.
She wore a flowered housedress accessorized
with a diamond necklace. My nine-year-old
impatience felt claustrophobic in adult company.

I strayed to her dilapidated barn where
I found a black lamb, a boxer named Bingo, and
the prototype of the most popular dog of the day,
Lassie. The animals followed me out of the barn
over field stubble. It still misted rain.
I was feeling damp and hungry, so I returned
to the house.

Three of Mom's six sisters had come with us.
The women huddled around the kitchen table,
laughed, talked incessantly until

their sounds became a kind of ongoing music.
Aunt Clara perched at the head of the table,
deemed matriarch by the rest of the family.

Slowly, that day and all of the rest of our visits
became the past that led to the moment
Dayton relatives found Aunt Clara in a coma
on the kitchen floor. She died that same day
in the Kettering hospital. Gone was the era.

GRANDMA MOHR

She broke green beans in half,
dropped them into a pot she held on her lap.
I knelt on a braided rug beside her, a handful
of beans, trying to do my part. I was twelve
years old, had chosen to stay with her
for a week where she lived
in a Buckeye-Lake cottage.

On the third day, she called me "thief."
I sprang to my defense, called her "impossible"
for accusing me of stealing rusty, fish hooks
from the basement. I bore guilt, wore it
like my best shirt because I was her favorite
grandchild, didn't want to lose her approval.
In this case she held a distorted view
of right and wrong. We shifted into silence
for the rest of the day. By day four, she
seemed to have forgotten my thievery.

Grandma collected everything:
rows of flower pots, receipts, countless
greeting cards. She hid money and jewelry
in drape linings, behind dresser drawers, and,
of course, under the mattress. A blood blister
on her lower lip poked out farther than usual
when she thought someone had looted her.

Every morning she hand-washed clothes,
hung them on a line in the grove,

puttered from dawn till sundown, took inventory
of her possessions like a suspicious child.

Each spring, she planted uneven rows
of vegetable seeds in a small plot of ground.
Things grew for her without much care.
It was as if her garden survived on magic
of her initial touch. She did try to ward off birds
from the tomato patch. A silver pie pan
tied by string to a tomato steak pulsed
in breezes like a scarecrow's heart.

Her children said she was crazy, blue bell,
cockle shell crazy, reciting rhymes learned
before dropping out of school after third grade.
Once or twice, relatives stopped talking about her
when I entered the room, so I never knew
if she hid cleverness inside mouthfuls of nonsense
or if sanity had slipped askew like a hat does
on a windy day.

Results of all her efforts seemed makeshift:
crooked pictures on flowered wallpaper, cotton stuffed
into screen door holes, Inventive? Old fashioned?
Wacky? Even as a child, I realized more
was going on than crippling, arthritic hands.

The afternoon she died, false teeth lay on the bed
beside her left shoulder. A trickle of saliva
had traveled down her wrinkled neck. Her eyes
resembled windows from which light had fled
leaving a hollow stare. She was barefoot,
and her toenails needed trimmed. I heard these
details from Mom.

The undertaker arranged her bones, powdered her
for eternity, placed her in a satin coffin between
two tourchiere lamps. They closed the lid on her
in May 1970.

I picture us again breaking beans in half,
hear the quick snap, hear songs she hummed
in a haphazard way, hear her call my Karmann Ghia
a buckboard, see her drop into the bucket seat.

Mostly, I feel guilty for affection withheld.
She would have rebuked physical closeness.
She never wrapped arms around anyone,
or kissed anyone. She was not a tender woman.
When I look back, I regret that I underrated her
as a person. That miscalculation compromises
conscience, feels like a switchbade
in my psychological gut.

GATHERING EGGS

Hinges squeak, hens squawk when
Grandpa Mohr opens the wooden door
to the chicken coop in the grove
behind the cottage at Buckeye Lake.
His boots stir straw dust on wooden floor.
Along the north wall, three rows of
identical roosts collect fragile bounty.
Many of the chickens crouch down farther
over their eggs. A few alarmed hens flap
to the floor like ineffectual sentries.
Grandpa empties each nest, places eggs
in a large bowl. Outside the hen house,
chicken protest reverberates upward
past treetops. Rinsing hands under outside
pump water, he barely hears continued clucks
of the robbed because of incipient deafness.

Each day, after working as a sign painter
of train cars at the Round House,
Grandpa trudges to the coop for eggs to help
sustain a wife, three sons, and seven daughters.
Reared in an orphanage tucked like a secret
in the hills of southern Ohio, his large family
warrants farming and raising chickens
to augment his day job. He treats his children
with severe discipline the same way workers
treated him in the orphanage.

Leaving the grove, re-entering the cottage,
he lays the bowl of eggs on the sink top.

Without indoor plumbing, he pumps again
from a hand-powered, water pump, fills a pot
for coffee, sips it before descending backstairs
to tools stored in a dirt-floor basement.
Retrieving the hand plow, he heaves it out
the door to side yard where he will work
in the garden until sun goes down
on commitment and cultivated dirt.

ANIMAL BURNS AND RED KISSES ON THE SNOW

Our boots crunch weed stubble in a two-acre field
a country block from Aunt Sarah and Uncle Peck's house.
I'm staying the week with them and my five cousins.
My uncle invites me to follow him into the cold,
December morning for a Saturday lesson in rabbit hunting.

We tramp over a foot of snow that lies like a white challenge
across the entire landscape. I follow in his tracks without a
weapon. He cradles a 22 caliber, rimfire rifle in the crook
of his arm. We wait for a rabbit to throw off hidden warmth.
I'm nine years old, feel privileged to accompany him.

Soon, a rabbit peeps from beneath a crust of snow.
Before I see the animal's movement take shape,
my uncle has raised his gun, stopped life with a single shot.
He hands the rabbit to me to carry by its feet.
Even with gloved hands, I feel it too much.
I keep its body half an arm's length away from mine.
Several times, I look to see if there is breathing.
Blood drips onto the snow like spots of liquid lipstick,
a conspicuous trail to this ornament of death.
I didn't want to kill. I wanted a small adventure
alongside my uncle, an outing toward manhood.

We trudge from the field, my distaste for hunting
as noticeable as the unwanted trophy I carry.

NO HOLIDAY

The tongue of leukemia laps at her strength
like a rabid dog. She is my neighbor, Bess,
who has come to visit and watch me decorate
the Christmas tree. "Each morning," she says,
"it takes me longer to get ready." I tell her
maybe the doctors are wrong. She received
her diagnosis yesterday. She tells me
her oncologist provided cold, comfortless advice,
told her not to despair. Her news sits in the room
with us like a third person, uninvited, unwelcome.

I plug in a string of lights, check for dark bulbs,
worn wiring. My hands reach deep into the
storage box. Fingers brush against several ornaments.
Grit of glitter rubs off. Sparkles, like hope, stick to skin
as I withdraw an orb with a hand-painted poinsettia on it.

I see her behind me in the ornament's reflection.
She waits for me to hang the first decoration in a vacancy.
I finish trimming the tree around midnight, walk her home
next door. It seems we must look at each other differently,
want answers to large questions that settle over us
like a smothering blanket.

Back home, I flop onto an overstuffed chair, gaze
at the tree's multicolored lights, remember how
truth slapped our brains with faithless chance
and false celebration.

SOOT ON THE SUN

Bearers lower Aunt Ada's coffin into the grave,
webbing slipping through their hands,
hand over hand. Family and friends straggle off,
group, regroup. I hold Aunt Liz's arm, tell her
this is where peace begins, aware of the green
canopy behind us. She stoops into the car. I linger
outside, watch a gravedigger lower the vault,
backhoe a mound of dirt into the hole.
Aunt Liz says she doesn't prefer to be
put in the ground, wants to be hung in a tree.
I asked what kind of tree? We laugh, allowing
this small joke. She wants to know if
we can visit family graves while in the cemetery.
Most of our family, except my parents,
have been buried here in Greenlawn.

The tallest yew tree I've ever seen shadows
her parents' grave. Natural Resources Department
registers the tree as 60 ft tall, 20 ft wide.
I have to bend my head all the way back
to see the top which is something I always do
when I visit my grandparents' grave.
Aunt Liz doesn't step from the car, so
I lower the window. She stares at the headstone,
her only comment that weeds need pulled.

Her husband, Uncle Toots, also lies near
a giant yew tree. Condition of his grave satisfies her.
We live together, and because she regards me

as her favorite nephew, I feel obliged to maintain
my uncle's plot. Again, she stares out the window
at the marker. She's ninety-four, and I can only guess
the irony in her head.

Before I start the engine, she turns to me, says,
don't forget the tree bit.

PART FIVE

CLAUSTROPHOBIC MARRIAGE

I liked your suit. You liked my hair.
Those dull words drew us into a marriage
of empty routines. Thousands of times
we rose from the same chairs. Mutual
considerations became as much
standard behavior as feeding ourselves.

Our marriage shrank to the size of a hand.
I heard our smothered screams
in all eight rooms, a relationship burned
down to the size of a cigarette butt
small enough to lose in the grass.

I planned to be the consummate wife,
but you immolated yourself with alcohol,
fell down stairs, broke your collarbone,
eyes looking out at nothing.

These days, I no longer hide truth
about space widening between us.
To think I was afraid to sew, afraid
you would see a habit you despised,
a fragment of my behavior that bothered.

At one time, you and I, a lawn, and
a garden meant everything. We have to spit
out the past like a wad of chewed tobacco,
accept that fields once surrounding our house
are overgrown with apartment buildings.

You see, I was tightening the lid on a Mason jar
the other day, autumn light blossoming
through the kitchen window, realized
we were both at the end. It was difficult
for me to tighten the lid. Nowadays, my wrists
are not as strong as when we married.
The kitchen smelled of tomatoes and fate.
I knew what it meant: I would pick up sewing
again, leave you to your beloved fields
that aren't even there anymore.

BURDEN OF DESPAIR

She pats her stomach, massages it
where life is forming. One night
on smooth sheets she gave herself
to him. What followed was the flash
of possession in her eyes. He promised
marriage, not yet fulfilled. Her breasts
have become heavier, hair glossier.
She walks a tightrope between delirious
expectation and a dubious tomorrow.
He hides regret, prances from room
to room with scornful eyes, still safe
in singleness. He doesn't want
a mother-in-law, son, daughter or a ghost
of the mistake he has made. He flops
into an armchair, glances at ceiling, beige
cleverness of Venetian blinds. Lamps,
tables, tangled designs on drapes press him
to question who are these things for?
Certainly not for him at twenty-five.
He's barely turned the corner from
adolescence, doesn't want to give up
freedom due him. Together, they victimized
yesterday's dreams, destroyed contentment.
Together, their throats move with unspoken
dialogue about the missing question of abortion.
Their wishes run in opposite directions
as she lights a Marlboro, and he flips the cap
on a bottle of Budweiser.

IN THE PRESENCE OF MICHELANGELO'S DAVID

David's magnificence would seem to warrant
mandatory silence in the Academia Gallery,

but shoe-shuffle sounds and discreet whispers
permeate admiration. People gaze at his body

as if giving homage to a god or as if enough
staring will let them permanently connect with

beauty. His veined hands, radial arteries
will never clog, ready as war to sling a stone

from a riverbed, wait forever for the right,
jubilant moment. He's an unbroken boy

bright with marble blood and celestial
illumination from a skylight above his head.

Tourists step as close as possible
to the contrapposto pose as if to reach a touch

past an observant guard before
their subconscious desire is discovered.

BOTTICELLI'S VENUS BECOMES A HOUSEWIFE ON THE FIRST DAY AFTER EMERGING

I look at coffee, realize I am
a morning person. I rest my head
against the pillow in a wingback chair,
stare out the window. Yellow sun seeps in.
Soon, I will reach for clothes, but not yet.

I linger in the shower, rinse away
remnants of sand, feel my way through the day,
answer a phone, read a book, wait
for purple sunset.

Eventually, I stand in the front yard,
watch April breeze bend daffodils.
When I re-enter the house, I open a window
for spring to enter, dress in sandals, blue shorts,
a sleeveless, white blouse. In the living room,
I reach under the sofa for a flat, brass box
in which I have stored remains of my shell.
Slouching in a chair next to a table on which
a radio sits, I tune through the spectrum
of adolescent woes until I filter in a Bela Bartok
concerto. I lounge and listen, wonder
if all houses are like this where a woman walks in
to be a wife and finds nothing but cats, clocks,
and cut glass, where love slips out the back door
in dirty socks for a five-minute haircut.

No one should take my myth for granted.
Was it a mistake to come here from the sea
and fret? Orpheus is not the only one weeping.
I am an immigrant who wants to turn her face
to another to worship. I eat, and no one
sits across the table from me. It is as if
someone left, and I read silences for clues
of his return. I regret I have left the shell,
place of my birth, the last thing in the sea
that ever touched me.

APPRAISING THE PARADE OF HOMES

People line up in July heat
in the admission's tent, purchase
a prepackaged welcome
and voyeuristic privileges.
They have come to look
at current trends in houses
and decor, cross each house's
threshold like homeless orphans
looking for half-open arms,
expectations sharpened to a point.

Green architecture and
eco-conscious living trend.
Designers covered chairs, sofas,
windows with finest-grade fabrics,
everything for being human
tucked out of sight. Good
Housekeeping would approve
of the simplistic elegance. Yet,
high style permeates.

These are not places to live
with chapped hands, runny noses.
Nothing as uninspired as comfort
has been included. Lupine, Gerber
daisies, zinnias in meticulous
flowerbeds thrive, apparently
unassailed by insects or garden tools.
Backyards connect as close as fingers

on a hand, no choice but to be
in the neighbor's palm, pressed near
to another person's privacy.

AUTOPSY

A vacuum sucks bone dust from the cranial cap.
High-pitch wine of the saw reverberates
from walls of the otherwise silent room.
Rib shears open the chest cavity. The mortician
extracts each organ. Her toothed forceps grip tissue.
A scalpel makes deeper cuts. Finished,
she replaces organs into the body cavity,
covers the decedent with a crisp, white, sheet.

Meanwhile, at home, family sip Merlot
and Pinot Noir, dust off old suits fitting
for a funeral, exchange platitudes.
Family cannot believe the dead stay dead,
do not rise from the cadaver cart
under fluorescent brightness, the exact spot
where each body part was examined
like a grammatical construction, and
nothing was left unnamed.
Family cannot believe they've heard the last
words from the tongue of the deceased
or that the hollow body lies under flimsy
shelter of an ordinary sheet.
Family cannot believe their loved one
does not feel the cold of the refrigerated drawer,
its complete silence, its impeccable ending.

DISMISSED

My German neighbor, Friedrich, lost his job
today. We both work as machinists
at the MMD Tool Company. He is an emigrant
from Wurzburg, still misses The Romantic Road
he says passes through astonishing landscapes.
He's had US citizenship for twenty years.
Cutbacks have cost him employment.
For most of those twenty years, we have carpooled.

This day, at quitting time, he slumps into my car
with the unfortunate news. I drive him home mostly
surrounded by silence, black lunchbox between us
like a sneer that says he will not show up at work
tomorrow. Once or twice, he glances at me,
a mental handshake of friendship. His large thumbs
rest on his lap. Silver-gray chest hair protrudes
from a blue, shirt collar. He exhales shallow breaths
as if he were in the process of disappearing.
I think he hides hostility in his gut, believes
he's being shoved aside for a younger person.
Even though he will receive severance pay,
an inelegant gesture, he says identity has been stolen.
I ache for him but suspect my own job is
in jeopardy too. It's as if a terrible twisting of
cylinders and cogs has jammed, seized this man's
meaning, dignity, and definition.

I drop him in front of his house. Once lush
lawn lacks water, sheathed in soot

from a nearby steel mill. He thanks me
as if nothing has changed, shakes my hand
like a stranger clutching at goodbye.
In my mind, I hear the broken sounds
he must utter as he enters the house
with white siding, shares the depth of his defeat
with a welcoming but unsuspecting wife.

STORY

I heard sirens, rushed to a front-room window
to see flashing, red lights. An emergency squad
parked in front of Mr. Dunning's house
foreshadowed bad news. Soon, EMTs hefted
a stretcher into the back of their vehicle. A white
sheet completely covered a body I assumed was
Mr. Dunning. It was the first neighborhood death
I had ever experienced. Mr. Dunning had one
elderly sister in a nursing home nearby. Otherwise,
he was without relatives. He dwelled two doubles
down from me. I never saw friends visit.
I imagined his sister wondering how to manage
her day despite crushing reminders of death's indignity.

Even though this was my first exposure to a neighbor
dying, it was all I needed to understand the clumsy end
that comes to everything that breathes.

Mr Dunning walked his Havanese several times a day,
never said hello, didn't socialize with other neighbors
from what I could tell.

I continued to loiter at the front window, watched
the grim summary of his life hauled away
to a funeral home, closed my eyes against a moment
I will never shrug off.

ROBERT'S HALLOWEEN

An all-day rain droops leaves that hang from limbs
like empty gloves. It's a five-star, autumn evening
luminous as a mirror. A particularly bright Hunter's
moon washes streets in silver light. Twelve-year-old
Robert lingers on his porch, wrinkles his forehead
to stop an itch behind a full-face, rubber, skull mask.
His trick or treat bag has a skull printed on it, too.
A candle glows yellow light inside a carved pumpkin
with a toothy grin. The pumpkin sits on porch railing
like an eerie sentry. Robert hears neighborhood chums
scamper around a corner, joins them.

They scurry from house to house, hungry
for as much candy as they can accumulate before curfew.
In the upsweep of excitement and movement,
they haven't noticed another boy has joined their group.
Buck, the class bully dressed all in black, wears a half,
wolf mask. He stays on the periphery until
a mischievous streak takes hold. His presence becomes
obvious when Robert feels a knee in his back. Jordan,
the huskiest one in the group, recognizes Buck
in spite of the mask, snatches Buck's bag of candy,
empties it into his own, then fits the empty bag
over Buck's head. The gang's uncontrollable laughter
rolls down the street. Jordan gives a push forward
that sends the Bully wobbling down the sidewalk.
In unison, the six boys break into a long, crying howl
that follows Buck until he's a block away from their
dauntless triumph.

THE LADY ON OUR STREET WHO SEWS DRESSES

I'm lying on my stomach in front of the console radio
listening to *Superman*. It's 1949, and I'm eight years old.
A knock at the door rouses me. Lucille, a black woman,
enters. A seamstress, she lives across the street
from our confectionery on Barthman Avenue,
sometimes does alterations on Mom's clothes. Today,
Lucille drapes a polka-dotted dress over her arm.
Mom escorts the twenty-five-year-old woman
to the kitchen where they sit at the wooden table.

Superman finished, I deepen concentration,
hear Lucille deliver details about the dress.
Mom has told me Lucille has perfect manners.
Lucille is neat and clean as freshly washed laundry
on a summer clothesline, always smells like lavender.
Petite as a plastic doll, she couldn't weigh more
than ninety-five pounds. It seems magical she can create
something to wear out of cloth and people's requests.
I wonder if she sews through the night without sleep?

I hear Mom open the cupboard where she keeps her purse.
Lucille thanks Mom, saunters through the living room
to the front door. Mom follows, thanks Lucille again.

I know Lucille is from a poor family, wears nothing
but homemade clothes. Her visit has reminded me
I want to give her my entire life savings
of twenty dollars in change. It disturbs me

picturing poor Lucille anchored to her sewing machine
past midnight, reaching out in the neighborhood
for the next job that will feed her mother and sister.

I turn off the radio in the middle of *Inner Sanctum*,
my throat dry with apologies and sadness.

A FRIEND WRITES TO ME ABOUT LIVING ALONE IN THE HOUSE IN WHICH HE WAS BORN

Ronnie paces oak floors in his circa 1850,
Kentucky farmhouse. His grandfather's
watch ticks in Ronnie's pocket. As if
he smells rain, he unfolds his mother's
wrinkled umbrella, ambles to the rural mailbox
where only bills have been deposited.
For no particular reason he thinks of his father,
a bricklayer, who plummeted from a scaffold,
hands grabbing air, grasping to no avail
for a hold on crooked sky. That death began
Ronnie's numerous dreams of resurrections.

He reenters the house, folds laundered sheets,
eyes the log pile through a window at the back
of the house, estimates if he has cut enough wood
for winter.

Late October chill permeates few remaining days
of unexpected warmth. He has asked himself if
living alone engenders a higher form of being
or simply removes him from the possibility
of connecting with other people. He hunts, fishes,
shops at Fillers Grocery located at the crossroads
in the middle of nowhere.

At night, he nestles beneath his grandmother's,
patchwork quilt that fluffs down over him
like a stranger's breath. It is in the dark,

before sleep, that losses come back to haunt.
Tonight, he wants more than isolation.
He wraps arms around a pillow, presses his face
into it without explanation, answers or apology.

AN INVENTED VISIT TO A PERSON WITH WHOM I HAVE EXCHANGED MANY PERSONAL LETTERS

I drive 300 miles in my imagination
to acknowledge a fan letter that names
your precise place of loneliness.
You've written of cattle and sheep
fenced on twenty acres of grassland
in Shelbyville, Kentucky, an estate
inherited from your parents.

I envision crossing state lines
on an impulsive, night drive to find you
as an answer to my own solitude.
I picture myself, trance-like, approaching
your door, unable to knock but looking
through a window that separates me
from a perfect friend. I would see
you folded into a chair by the fireplace,
pensive face reflecting orange glow
of burning logs. I would wish to become
visible, but fear of rejection would shudder
me like Arctic air. I would taste October
moonlight on my tongue, the tang of longing.
When I look over shadowy pastures,
I would stay hidden in night as if wearing
a hunter's camouflage. Through the window,
I would continue to watch you doze,
shoulders slumped. I would never knock,
return to my car, afraid you won't offer
an invitation for intimacy.

THREE-DIMENSIONAL ESCAPE

SKY

He looks up as if he has never seen sky before,
clouds shaded in pink. He has succumbed to
staring higher than everyday air.
Where would birds go if there weren't sky?
He watches a flock of geese swoop into formation
as if following an invisible plan. They will sleep
on water, afraid of predators on land. If he had
bird bones, he, too, would soar to the end of the sky
away from instinctual fear and dangerous dreams.

EARTH

Inside his house, he breathes uneasy, switches on a lamp.
Light spreads over ragweed-colored carpet.
He snaps on a radio, an old trick for adding additional life
to an empty place. Coldplay's "Viva La Vita" floods
the speaker. Accepting the illusion that the whole world
is singing, he glances at bookshelves, remembers
he has already read the best books. As if working from
a blueprint, he dawdles through routines, stands in the middle
of the living room, shocked to be human, wondering
what truths he has missed. He listens to the far away assurance
of the radio, but if he had wings like geese, he would glide
into the huge sky away from insufferable isolation.

THE BLACKSMITH'S EXHIBIT

The man splashes sparks off Anvil,
sinks hot iron into water that sizzles.
I'm part of a crowd squeezed into a tent
at the Pickaway County Fairgrounds.
The middle-age blacksmith has brown,
curly hair. His exhibition fascinates,
mesmerizes. I think of horse-drawn wagons
as I watch him pull a metal strip from hot coals.
He pinches it between tongs, slides it
onto the anvil in one smooth move.
His flat-head hammer shapes something
mysterious out of orange fire. He never once
glances up as if to do so would breach
authenticity. Repeated blows flatten metal
into a recognizable bracelet. The little stall
barely accommodates his height. A bit of
theatricality surfaces when he turns
to pump billows. He's definitely on stage
for an enthralled, enthusiastic crowd.
I sense a slight insinuation of sensuality
in this process of forging from fire.
Is that why I watch with rapt attention
because this man's sinewy arms compensate
for lack of love? The smithy's strength crests
with last hammer blows to tease out jewelry,
possibly to compensate for repressed desire.

BELLIGERENCY AT BURGER KING

It starts as a trickle of discontent,
escalates into a flood of hostility.
The manager stands at the top
of an aisle behind the counter,
her employees stunned by her
quarrelsome outburst.
She spits intolerance, furious
employees are getting
orders wrong and arguing.
Her temper rockets to hysteria,
screams an unintelligible version
of her mother tongue. I huddle
at a table, eating cold french fries,
worried I'll be caught in the crossfire.

Even as she delivers an order
to a customer in the parking lot,
she rages with an incomprehensible tongue.

Returning, she retraces steps
across the dining area, screeching
anger all the way. One of the employees
trudges from behind the counter, slumps
at a table, bullied and browbeaten.
I don't know if he is the cause of the uproar,
but suddenly, quiet descends like
a conciliatory net dropped over the whole
group of employees.

When I think it safe, I order a Whopper
without meat. The manager gawks,
mouth flapped open in disbelief, says
they're out of wrappers, could she
put the sandwich into a sack? I wait,
nervous the storm will resurface.
She plops the sack onto the counter.
I open it, examine contents, see pickles,
onions, cheese, mayonnaise, lettuce, tomato,
and much to my vegetarian horror,
a slice of beef. Moreover, there is no bun
around these contents. No bun!
I'm flabbergasted, unwilling to risk
her anger by reordering.

I drop the sack into the trash, scoot out
to my car, hungry but glad to escape
another upheaval.

Though disgusted, all the way home
I cackle, laugh that there was no bun,
just a sack of condiments
conducive to a do-it-yourself sandwich.

A LETTER OF DESPAIR

On a backcountry road it's raining
upon abandoned debris: squashed,

milk cartons, faded, lottery tickets
crushed, beer cans, cigarette butts,

bits of windshield glass. It's as if
apathy were a hitchhiker who had

emptied pockets while waving
a thumb in the air. Disregard

for housekeeping the land is
as omnipresent as roadside billboards.

Beyond these things, even hawks
do not drift down to, Holsteins feed

far into the fields away from man's
carelessness. Drizzle glistens

on farmhouse roofs, tops of silos,
barn cupolas. Questions persist:

what compels people to give thanks
for the world this way? What kind of

cold distance separates them from
respecting their own earth?

Rain increases, obfuscates air
and fast-food litter that lies

along berms like reminders
of irresponsible neglect.

THE MYTH OF MOZART'S COMMON GRAVE

Wrapped in cheesecloth,
the cheapest kind of shroud,

trundled to the cemetery
by a horse-drawn hearse,

his corpse slides
from an unpainted box

into a muddy grave.
The thud it makes

as it lands atop the pile
of other anonymous bodies

is absorbed by relentless rain.
A gravedigger throws a few

shovelfuls of quick lime
into the hole, sky's lingering

darkness the only benediction.
Perfect pitch, still in the brain,

has been turned upside down,
washed of passion,

in what was previously
a cornfield.

A SMALL HISTORY OF LIFE ON ANOTHER PLANET

A pilot astronaut, graduated
from the University of California, I lounge
near a casement of my spacecraft, Cressida,
tempted to open the acrylic window to inhale odor
of space, an acrid smell like walnuts and brake pads,
gunpowder, burnt almond cookies. This is the last
trip I will ever take because I'm going to Uranus
where I cannot land, but if I could, I'd have only
one second to breathe. It is a pilgrimage to death,
a suicidal sacrifice for a glimpse of pure beauty.

I lean back, gaze at elegance and grace
of the solar system. I am one billion miles from
earth, have .6 to go.

When I reach my destination, I hang
above the outer envelope of molecular hydrogen,
helium, and methane. I stare at the airlock, now
a door to eternity, a state of existence outside of time.
Minus 320° Fahrenheit presses against the ship.
Bone-breaking cold ices windows. Though
no chance for survival exists without a DNA remapping,
I choose the dream despite terror of reality.

I open the airlock. Fifteen seconds later,
space enfolds my body, buries me
in a rain of diamonds.

www.ingramcontent.com/pod-product-compliance
Lightning Source LLC
Chambersburg PA
CBHW022156160726
48282CB00024B/218
* 9 7 8 8 1 1 9 6 5 4 8 6 4 *